Willow Books, the Poetry Imprint of

AQUARIUS PRESS
Detroit, Michigan
www.willowbookspoetry.com

Psalm of the Sunflower

Cover Art: David Warren, warrend@hsu.edu

Author Photo (back cover): Allen Loibner

ISBN 978-0-9819208-6-3
LCCN 2009934319

Willow Books, the Poetry Imprint of
AQUARIUS PRESS
PO Box 23096
Detroit, MI 48223
(313) 515-8122
www.willowbookspoetry.com
aquariuspress@sbcglobal.net
www.aquariuspressbookseller.net

Printed in the United States of America

for my grandmother, Marilyn Dee Williams Henry

Table of Contents

Foreword

I often end a letter to friends by reminding them to continue to walk in the light. It's an expression that is probably an outgrowth of my reading sacred texts. In this book that unfolds in front of you, Antoinette Brim describes herself as a sunflower, *"dark the uncovered petals peeled back."* She tells us that all she needs is the light. In some ways Brim's work seems to follow and uphold the tradition given to us by Jean Toomer and Lucille Clifton. What one expects from these writers is not a simple examination of racial identity but instead a testimonial of what is righteous and spiritually instructive. Consider how the lilies of the field grow. One reads to the "brim" with the understanding that this woman is from good people.

I like when Antoinette Brim writes about her mother and captures the lessons taught and the ones learned.

Mother was never more beautiful
than when she sang with Lady Day
playing on the turntable.
Her back supported by the doorframe,
her arms crossed at her breasts,
her long slender fingers holding a cigarette stained Ruby Red.

One turns to poetry not just for remembrance but for details. I need to see Brim's mother holding a cigarette. Remember when smoking was an act of defiance? In **Psalm of the Sunflower**, Brim shares with us her inheritance and the power of red lipstick. In "A Glimpse of Minnie" we see her mother-in-law succumbing to cancer but not before we find her breathing in the fragrance of flowers. In the poetry of Antoinette Brim one will find the celebration of life inside the darkness of reality. And, here lies the blues and the light Brim wants us to reach with longing.

Psalm of the Sunflower will take your hand and lead you outdoors. How beautiful is Little Rock, Arkansas? Brim is at her best when we find her *"...waiting beneath the sweet chestnut trees."* It is nature that knows our true secrets, the poet only confesses. What happens when a poet tells us to travel to the edge of jazz? Antoinette Brim writes with sweet language in her mouth. On the tip of her tongue a taste of mango. Poems leave her hands to fly with robins, crows and nightingales.

Bridges were once burning in Arkansas, but somehow we continue to move from one place to another. We cross over because good poetry is a path. Follow the words of Brim and you will find no boundaries, just the light revealing itself and measuring the distance traveled. When blues turn into psalms we not only know why the caged bird sings, we also know the song of life required to heal the broken wing. While William Carlos Williams writes about a red wheelbarrow, Brim suggests we consider the meaning behind a coat thrown over the back of a chair.

Folks say we don't see many black flowers. I hope no one overlooks Antoinette Brim. In this first book she blossoms, stretches and reaches the sun. I don't really need to tell you this—so, let me hush now and don't explain. Here is a new book of poems that might make you beg for more.

E. Ethelbert Miller
Washington, D.C.
February 15, 2009

Acknowledgments

Grateful acknowledgment is made to the editors of the following journals and anthologies in which these poems first appeared: "Tell me," *The Drunken Boat;* "Freedom is Red," *The November 3rd Club;* "Burning Bridges," *Just Like A Girl: A Manifesta;* "Cherry Blossoms," "Eve," "In the Lions' Den" and "Why a Flower Dresses in Black," *The View from Here;* "The Power of Red Lipstick" and "A Glimpse of Minnie," *Signifyin' Harlem*; "The Poet is Freed," *Cave Canem Anthology, Volume #6*; "Forcing It (then titled *Letting Go Wish*)," *Riverwalk.*

Thank you to E. Ethelbert Miller for blessing my book with its beautiful forward. Thank you to David Warren for the gift of his art, which graces the book's cover. My deepest gratitude to my teachers and mentors: David Clewell, Reta Madsen, Ruth Forman, Chris Abani, Peter Levitt, Eloise Klein Healy, Cornelius Eady, Toi Derricotte, Patricia Smith, Cyrus Cassells, Ralph Burns, Kwame Dawes, Elizabeth Alexander, Quincy Troupe and Major Jackson. I am honored to thank the Cave Canem Foundation, its faculty and fellows, for their support and tutelage. I give my heartfelt thanks to the Antioch University MFA program (where this manuscript began), its faculty and my cohorts. Thanks also go to the Fine Arts Work Center in Provincetown and the Archie D. and Bertha H. Walker Foundation Scholarship that made my attendance possible. I am humbled to have the love and support of my dear friends: Niki Herd, Demetrice Worley, Lita Hooper, Lesa Jordan, Doug Hoffman, Garbo Hearne, Shareese Kondo, Darius Williams, Bernadine Cartagena, Fanon Wilkins, Vicki Tanner, Ulrike White, David Warren, Robin Griffith and John Willis.

Thank you to my children: Roland-Michael, Waverly and Thomas who inspire me to be my best self. Thank you to my brother, Anthony, who has known me always and loved me always. Thank you to Randall Horton, my forever love. Most of all, I give a very special thank you to my grandmother, Marilyn Dee Williams Henry, for her love, dedication, and unwavering support.

Forcing it

When the magnolia trees began dropping
their flowers out of season, I knew
it was time to let you go, but
old folks say, *shock a branch – make*
it bloom, with plastic wrap
water in a jar,
a little light
enough time –
some space –
wait.

Freedom is Red

For Argument's Sake

Just suppose you'd missed the exit
didn't swing around wide into the parking lot
in that red Firebird. Suppose I didn't
hear the last strains of Tracy Chapman's
Fast Car spilling from your half rolled down window
and then halted abruptly by the turn of your ignition key.

Suppose you didn't sit in my section and I hadn't suggested
the bacon chili cheeseburger and you hadn't winked
and taken my word for it. Suppose you hadn't written
your name and number on the dollar bill you left for a tip.
Suppose I'd figured you for a cheap bastard and
bought a newspaper and some gum instead of calling you.

Suppose you weren't home. Suppose you didn't have an
answering machine or Southwestern Bell Call Notes.
Suppose I hadn't taken down the directions correctly.
Suppose I'd missed the gravel road half hidden behind
lilac bushes grown wild. Suppose I hadn't followed that road,
gravel popping and crunching under my tires, shooting up like
buckshot, dinging my paint, smoky dust rising in my rear view mirror.

A small house by the sea

She wants to feel clean,
so everyday she does laundry
separates face cloths
from the underwear.

She wants to be a good mother, so
the kids are always hugged and kissed.
Always on time to
soccer
dance
piano
karate
and still,

she wants to be a good wife, so
at half past six, dinner appears on the table
heat rising off the roast and mashed potatoes.
There's bacon in the green beans. Fresh tea
crackles the ice and lemon wedges
float near the rim of the glass.

He wants to be successful,
so sometimes he is late—
greets her with a quick kiss
fingering her breast like loose change.

She sometimes thinks of leaving
but only recently finished decorating the house.
Everything has a place. She's put
everything in its place. How could she
take it all apart, pack it all away. Where
would she go anyway, though she longs
for a small house by the sea. A place
all her own, where she can look out
at the water and get a sense of forever.

And when her freshly showered, warm body
slips between the cool cotton sheets and seeks
out the heavy wall that is his sleeping body;
when she fits herself around the curve of his back
presses her lightly glossed lips to the nape of his neck
over and over until he wakes, she knows

she is trading her body for a moment
of undivided attention, a gentle good morning kiss
the morning after. An extra fifty in her allowance. Perhaps
a knock at the door in the afternoon, she'll answer
to find a delivery man bearing roses.

Menarche

life spills out of me
as spools of thin red ribbon tossed
from high windows
unravel

Eve

What if the apple was metaphor

not for knowledge
or temptation
but maybe, it was all about Eve

how she offered herself to Adam
how he took her into his hands
marveled at her smooth roundness
sank his teeth into her flesh

maybe it's just a cautionary tale

a warning against being
pared back
quartered
cored?

In the Lions' Den

– in memory of Teresa

I.

If God had not closed the lions' mouths,
I wonder how long Daniel would have lasted.
How long would the lions have circled, slinked
shaking the dust from their manes and roaring.

How long before Daniel's knees weakened,
his bladder fainted, leaking water?
Could he have bought himself time –
ripped one finger, then another
from his trembling hands, and
thrown them to the circling lions?
Offered up his arm, his leg –
to save his beating heart?

II.

How much time did you lose
that night, baking brownies for a Bible study,
you were too sick to attend.

The stars were out.
We could have counted them
together, perhaps renamed them
for the children you would leave behind.

III.

Queen Esther was wise. She knew to wait quietly.

Wait

to be invited into her husband's presence,
kneel by his throne. Knowing her place
saved her life and the lives of her people.

Esther knew
she was in the lions' den.
Esther knew
how to get out.

IV.

The handfuls of hair shed from the root
didn't send you to the doctor—
your swollen hands, swollen feet—
your face covered in hair fine as down
didn't send you.

He didn't send you.

V.

Some nights, the roaring keeps me from sleeping
keeps me from eating, keeps me from writing—

The business you never opened; the children you never raised.
We could have counted the stars together.

The laundry, the dishes, the poem in my head—
How long did Esther wait, kneeling at the throne?

For Teresa

In lieu of flowers,
I send rain to soften grief—
wash away regret.

Freedom is Red

The first time I asked a man for a divorce, the Challenger exploded.
It wasn't my fault, but seventeen years later, I'm divorcing again
and the Columbia is lost. I wonder if it is wise to send up another shuttle.

On the stretch of tape not damaged by heat,
the Columbia astronauts are laughing. Happy to be
seconds from home. When the tape ends, the newscast cuts to video
of streaks of burning shuttle. Two arcs of light in the sky.

My daughter wants to show me a video she found in my bedroom.
It's a tape of her brother's 5th birthday party. She is only three months old,
asleep in my mother's lap, as squealing five-year-olds in cowboy hats,
wearing tin sheriff stars on their T-shirts munch gummy worms they pull
from Oreo dirt pie. She says I was the happy Mommy back then.

Afterwards, I watch the news. See the bombs falling on Baghdad.
Arcs of light illuminating mosques and marketplaces.
Stars to be wished upon. I am afraid because
Thelma's son is there and Ann's is on the way.

The president says we must free the people of Iraq. It must be done.
It makes no sense to me. My divorce makes no sense to my daughter.
That I must split us to make things better. I tell her some things
she is too young to understand. I will explain them when she is older.
I pray I will have an answer for her by then.

So when I go to court, the judge will ask me what systems failed.
I'll mumble something about shields and pressure and heat.
He'll want to know if I could see it coming and I'll say,
I thought something fell away at launch, but wasn't it supposed to?
Like when I was five and we watched the first men fly into space
on their way to the moon. Didn't the rocket break apart?
Didn't a fireball fall to earth? He'll tell me
that was the old way.

When Baghdad falls, where will it land? Who will be left to be free?
When all of the bombs have burst in mid-air. When the red plumes a
burned to ash and cinder. To which victor will the spoils go?
If I get the table and he gets the chairs, should the children
stand over the table or sit plate in hand? Does it matter now
which one of the thousands of shields failed?

A Flock of Dragonflies

Blues Haiku

down so low, don't think
I can get up. down so low,
don't believe in up.

A Glimpse of Minnie

–for Minnie Brim

It's been nearly four years since you left me in the November pre-daw
with no one to clean greens with, no one to discuss
how okra gets tough when it grows fatter than your finger.
Somehow I believe I should mark the occasion.
I just haven't figured out how.
Something tells me, I should do something irreverent–
Maybe take down that country-red-door welcome flag
from my front porch flag pole and
tie on our wonder bras,
the ones that we bought on our ladies' day out,
the bras we had to wear out of the store.
We arched our backs and swung our hips.
You said that I could put someone's eye out.
I stopped to salute yours.

I caught a glimpse of you
a while ago at the farmer's market,
your back was to me.
I bumped and excused myself
through the crowd to reach you.
You were bent over so far, your face was nearly buried
in the cut flowers. You were breathing in so deeply
I could hear the air being drawn into your nostrils.
Even before I could see your face, I knew your eyes were closed.
I smiled, then laughed and took your arm,
but your face belonged to someone else
and I remembered that you are gone. It seems a waste
to buy cut flowers when you are not here.
Who else could appreciate the sacrifice they make,
giving themselves so totally?

I made greens last week. Not like we made them,
driving out to meet the farmer on Tuesdays,
choosing the greenest, most fragrant leaves,

some collard, some mustard.
Stooping down to peer into the butcher's glass case
for the meatiest hamhocks. Then laughing on the drive home.
But it wasn't like our Tuesdays when we spent all afternoon
soaking greens, picking greens, tossing tough stems into
water-spotted brown paper sacks. On our Tuesdays,
we filled the house with the smells of greens and hamhocks simmering
in deep, black pots for hours, while you told me stories of your Mother –
her hair tied in a kerchief, calling instructions to you over her shoulder
about the little ones she left in your care. Your mother
rushing toward the sound of the honking horn,
hoisting herself into the truck filled with black faces &
kerchiefed heads on their way to waiting white cotton fields.
Not our Tuesday, just a canned greens Tuesday.
Forgive me.

You survived the first summer on a diet of greens and cornbread,
neck bones, ox tails, shark cartilage and chemotherapy.
As the air turned cold, you suggested we plant
pansies and mums in purple and gold. I was proud
of our handiwork until the mums began to die back
and I couldn't coax them into blooming again.
I felt slighted and assured you that I wouldn't plant mums again.
You reminded me of this the following fall, as we again planted
pansies and mums in purple and gold.
They died back again, before I was satisfied.
The next fall, you watched me from the porch step
with that cancer rag on your head
and a weak smile on your lips.

I walked through the garden
after your memorial service
when the guests had eaten and gone home.
The mums had died by then.
As I cut them back, I realized
I had asked too much of them.
They had done what they were made to do.

I caught a glimpse of you today
when your son and grandson climbed into
the red club chair, the one you settled into and died.
They watched television until they fell asleep,
their heads tilted back, their mouths jutting open
just like you did each evening
your bare feet on the ottoman,
your wig slipping back on your head just a bit—
eyes closed, mouth open until we shook you gently
and helped you back to bed.
You looked just like that the morning you died.
When the paramedics came to the house, I wanted to say:
She's just asleep in the chair.

A Flock of Dragonflies

Souls waiting to be reborn are transformed into dragonflies. A flock of dragonflies forecasts rain.
– saying from India

Must one die to receive wings?

The air is burnt
the grass is brittle underfoot.

Bring me rain
violent, crushing

cooling rain.

Have you come to shake your
wings in my face,
demand I stand
again?

Flocks of dragonflies
dizzy me,

more storms coming?

I'd lay it all down
for iridescent wings.

It all comes down to a simple blue suit

– for my Uncle Billy

A double-breasted blue suit with a finish slick as polished lapis. Creased pants, pressed sure & straight as a contractor's snapped chalk line. A silk blue tie flecked with sunlit gold is draped across a striking white shirt muted by thin blue lines. Elegant. Simple.

Remember my Easter Dress. Ice pink crepe. Shimmering like frost on the mall parking lot. It had a v-neck. Large black buttons. A wide patent leather belt to cinch my young waist. It was a fine dress. From a fine store. And oh, I felt so fine.

The sales associate pulls handkerchiefs from the display, lays them across. He watches my eyes, speaks in hushed tones. White silk, too stark. Gold, too cheerful. I motion to a simple blue handkerchief.

I'd come home in a hurry to hide. To crawl into my Nana's bed. Be a child again instead of a wounded wife. Shed tears as luminous as the icicles pulled to the concrete patio floor by their frozen weight. And when the first too thin robin returned to the thawing Pennsylvanian landscape, you took me to the mall to buy an Easter dress. My adored uncle, with a pocket full of paycheck -- on a mission to make me smile.

I run my hand across this double-breasted blue suit. A funeral suit with a finish slick as polished lapis. The suit you will wear into eternity. I feel you over my shoulder, but I can't see you. Can only feel the store heater blowing in my face, the tears cutting into my cheek, the roughness of the Kleenex scraping against my nose. I am in the salesman's arms now, sobbing from a place so deep all that rises into the air is echoes.

And in an instant, I am in the mall parking lot. We are young. Tip-toeing from blacktop to blacktop, around the islands of ice. What are we laughing about? Why are we eating ice cream in the winter? Why are we carrying so many bags? My Easter dress, two pairs of shoes. We are so fine. A fortune teller and her daughter miss the last bus, and look fearfully out into the dark street. You smile at me, and we take them home, follow them into a parlor where they read our palms and they tell us stuff we can't share for thirty days. And we laugh, because we don't believe a word they say, but we want to because it all sounds so good. They say we'll find love, we have to be patient, they say we'll be blessed. But they never say they see a blue suit. Never say, it will all come down to a simple blue suit.

planting mums and pansies in the rain

plant drizzles of watercolor
in purple and gold

dragonflies over head
name the blue one Teresa

the tiger-striped,
Uncle Billy

cool dirt
pansy petals soft

baby Victoria
is a pink dragonfly

once barren flowerboxes
are suddenly abloom

storms drape the sky
in robes of purple mourning

day will not break
though the clock chimes dawn

The Deep

The sea cucumber is no fool

it spews its guts
when threatened

then swims away

leaving its assailant in a tangle
of entrails and emotion.

***

A jellyfish has no heart

its filmy opalescence
entices a gentle caress

which it rewards
with a terrible sting.

***

The ocean rushes up

greets me with a moist kiss of breeze
drapes my feet in lacey foam.

and like a fool, I release

the skirts of the shoreline
and am drawn into the deep.

Many Waters

"Many waters cannot quench love, neither can the floods drown it"
– Song of Solomon 8:7

You cannot drive the 430 River Bridge twice.
Every morning, it is new.
On Mondays, while mourning
the loss of a weekend sacrificed
to housework,

I've flown across
into a haze   so heavy   so thick
there is no horizon ahead
and no road that lies behind.

I've punched through
morning dove gray mist
that caresses the quarry rock below,
this vaporous façade
of a safe place to fall, but
it's all rushing water
beneath.

Abruptly
the river descends 5,000 feet
falling into an ashen cushion
of gray velvet shimmers.

I've met the river on my terms:
on the dock to feed the ducks
at the Café for a coffee
at festival to watch it snuff out
spent shells of fireworks – those
variant flashes of fallen hue.

Clinging to rusty rails, I've leaned
over this river, my ears filled with the sound
of crashing currents dissolving
into watery communion.
The river knows my name.
It calls me to the edge
where there are no rusty rails.
It calls to me on amazing Monday mornings like this,
when the car is filled with the best of the 80's
and it's good news about gas prices.

It calls up to me on the 430 River Bridge
and asks me about you. I answer:

River, we were not enough. He has betrayed us for Ocean.

Burning Bridges

The newsman says
someone is going around burning bridges in Arkansas—
        historic bridges, old covered wood bridges
        some bridges dating back to the Civil War.

I suspect you
turning history into loss, turning
time into a torch that can't be passed.
You got this thing for burning bridges.
Can't wait for decay, for termites
for quiet erosion.

So, I reckon it's you
in the quiet of night,
begging crickets to keep still,
daring deer to let the moonlight
cast glints of moonbeams in their eyes.

It's you
dry twigs crackling underfoot
stealing away to burn Arkansas bridges.

See, bridges are there for a reason
for getting you on from one place to another.
And the thing is, once you've crossed a bridge
nothing says you got to go back across it.

But you burn bridges you might
want to cross again sometime.
You ain't thought it through, and you won't
until you choke on your own smoke
until you are smudged with your own ash.

Then you'll stand knee deep in cold, hostile river water
fierce enough to drag you in its undertow.

Yeah, it's you
burning Arkansas bridges in the still of night.
You got this thing for
dramatic finality.
You got this thing for the mournful
cries of mourning doves sent off course
by the grey smoke of burning bridges.

You'd choke the song out of a swallow
to sit in your own silence
and pout
about what you lost
on the other side of the river.

Exit Signs

At the Andina Café by the Riverfront,
the vets gather to sip coffee and bum cigarettes.
One asks me for seventy cents for a pound of apples.
I hand him four quarters and the bag
of chips that came with my sandwich.
You're good people, he tells me.
The hum of distant traffic competes
with the muffled voices of vets.
I sit with my back to the river
because it calls to me.

When love dies in autumn

Boundaries

I.

A hedge of cream-colored honeysuckles
bordered the Center Elementary School softball field.
The blossoms strained against their boundaries, insistently
reaching through the diamond spaces of chain link
to find our tiny hands and mouths.
We spun in circles, winding ourselves
in honeysuckle scent until
we fell down dizzy.

II.

I loved you once
with a love as wild as honeysuckles
no chain link fence could contain.

III.

Fences are good. If you know which side to stand on.
There was a time when I could reach through the fence, when
my hands were small enough to slip back through with a fistful
of blossoms. I knew bumblebees hid in honeysuckles. But
there was no fear, I trusted myself.

Now, fearing the sting, I bury my fists deep in my pockets.
Still, I smell honeysuckles. Their scent is as thick as a wall,
only the ghost of my innocence can pass through.

In the Gilded Cage

She's grown quite
comfortable, her wings
losing their buoyancy
long ago.

Still there's a certain pleasure in the
predictability of a sturdy perch
that swings far enough forward
to make her stomach flutter
and back again
where she knows she's safe.

Her water is measured. Enough
to douse her wings, lay them smooth;
enough to sip with her seeds
rolled in peanut butter, though

she dreams of cherries so ripe
they bleed from the gentlest nibble.

Wings

After you broke my wing,
I tucked my head deep in my downy feathers

while you scratched stones into the air
to rain down like brimstone.

So absorbed in your cackling,
you failed to notice the healing:

beak turning talon,
the widening breadth of my wingspan,

not until I lifted into the air
your cackles silenced by distance.

Tell me

The gas is off
our children are cold.
Do you love me?
I heat water in the microwave to fill
the sink to wash their faces and hands.
Do you love me?
I sit up with the space heater
watching for sparks. Our children
are barely lumps under layers of quilts.
Your love leaves me cold
leaves me hungry
leaves me.
Enough becomes less when divided
into three small mouths. I've grown
too old, too practical for promises.
Sing sweet songs that rise on the steam
of pots of boiling potatoes. Look at me
with soft eyes as the furnace awakens with a roar.
When our children run past me in bare feet,
white cotton t-shirts grazing their thighs,
then I will know you love me.

Your coat confided in me

how you threw it across the back of a chair,
rumpled, half inside out and in danger
of slipping to the floor.

This Old Thing

I will have worn them once or twice maybe three times,
before I let you see me in them. I scrape the shoes on the sidewalk.
I wash the jeans until they feel soft, until their colors grow muted.

I shred price tags.

When love dies in autumn

The leaves rustle like whispers she is not meant to overhear,
like her lover on the telephone, his muted whispers
spilling into the ear of another.
It doesn't take much to shake dead leaves from their trees.
She says go.
He doesn't silence her,
doesn't press his lips hard against hers.
Just slips on his jacket. Sulks out.
She walks the dog in the dimming evening light.
The October wind, like his mistress, is invisible, but in her face:
blowing her off balance   roaring in her ears   numbing her.
Funny how she never noticed
the leaves turning,
just one morning they were red and gold.
She wonders when it happened.
When the leaves actually died;
if they knew they were dying
and if the letting go
was painful.

In Response to Your Letter

Your words chase me like schoolyard
bullies. I want to shove back.

Had you sent me silence,
I would have waited patiently for
your love to return

but these words,
release me.

Sometimes

I have no words left,
just the steam rising
from a hot bath and a song
that spills from an old stereo.
That singer—
she's found the words
lost to me.

<u>Unrequited</u>

Why a flower dresses in black

We do not see many black flowers. In 1939, one was reported to be growing in northern Oaxaca, Mexico. Fifty years later, a botanist went in search of the flower (*Lisanthius nigrescens*). No one knows what pollinates this flower. No one knows why a flower would dress in black.

—Sharman Apt Russell, *Anatomy of a Rose*

I am the flower who dresses in black, who hides itself away
whose head lists low, wilting for the want of you.
I drop pollen like teardrops, close my petals
to sit shivah; send up fragrance like incense to honor
what is lost. I am the near invisible shimmer
of black satin in the night wind.

It is safer to hide away. To make love seek
one out. To answer questions, only after
they have been asked.

A fractured heart spews life with each futile beat, first red
so red, then violet, but it all dries black. Glistening pools
of coal oil that in time painful pressure will turn to diamond.
It is that way with all beauty.

Pollen teardrops caught on the merciful coolness of breeze
will land on my lips, a kiss blown by a lover I cannot see
spawns a promise of rejuvenation. A blossom of hope

never to be pinned to a shoulder or tied at the wrist.

I will die in dark places. Drop petals the wind will cover
in deep earth that remembers a time all others have forgotten.

Cherry Blossoms

I.

Each spring I would sweep the tiny wild cherries off the driveway
before the children stomped them into purple stains on the concret
It was years before I realized they were good to eat.
I enjoyed them one spring. The next year,
the yard man came.

II.

I knew the tree would die, I told the yard man
but he wouldn't hear me. He only smiled. Assured me he knew hi
business.
While I was away, he cut through her cord of root to save the sidewa
By morning, her leaves had withered. *Shock,* he said. *She will recove*

She dropped her leaves before autumn. Stood naked through the wir
Failed to clothe herself in blossoms that spring. The returning robir
could not nest in her branches. She was dead inside. She had been f
some time.

III.

I dreamt her in full bloom, heavy with white linen blossoms.
I awakened into air thick with the promise of dark, wildly sweet cher
But as I walked to the window, the tree washed away
like a child's lost watercolor dropped
to the sidewalk
in the rain.

Unrequited

Night unfolds
its indelible black screen.
A quiet separation.
Day and Night
once laced together
are now loosed
by a knowing Wind
whose hushed laughter
invites the cricket night song—
their melodic chants swim naked
through the darkness. The Wind parts
his mouth moist with river sprays
but Day drapes herself in quiet robes
of washed purple twilight
and is gone.

(You got me) begging like Billie

I'll attend your wedding this summer in a yellow sundr
bare shouldered with my slipped-out-of sandals tied
by their satin ribbon ankle straps slung over one shoulder
my freshly manicured toes nuzzling the newly cut lawn

your summer wedding set to the coo of captive doves color washe
in lilac and lavender me in a lemon yellow sundress its meringue
outstretched catching breeze; there will be so much you want to say
but there won't be time not this time

Hush now, don't explain

Funny how some things you can see afar off a train wreck you can't a
So, you give yourself to it open up to the crash and bang of it
feel yourself roll with it wondering all the time if this ti
you'll live through it

And you know that I love you
And when love endures,
right and wrong don't matter
I'm so completely yours

But Baby, its only spring time now butterflies are yet cocooned
tadpoles are still swimming in their big frog dreams Baby, everyt
has a season ain't time yet for no yellow sundr

Try to hear folks chatter
And I know you cheat
Right or wrong don't matter
When you with me, Sweet

Your kisses refresh me like Big Mama's sun tea
set out to steep in the window box strange how it
seems all the sugar settles at the bottom sometimes
when you get to the end it tastes too sweet

Hush now don't explain
What is there to gain

Your sleepy hand draped lazy 'cross my thigh
seems right in morning light

Just say you'll remain
Rising sun don't mean nothing   it rises every morning   let it rise
on you here   tomorrow   and the next day   and the day after that

Just say you'll remain

No need to   grope for apologies   grope for lies

And *you know that I love you*
And when love endures,
right and wrong don't matter
I'm so completely yours

I *hear folks chatter*
And I know you cheat
Right or wrong don't matter
When you with me, Sweet

Hush now, don't explain
Just say you'll remain

My life's your love
Don't explain

Song lyrics from *Don't Explain,* as sung by Billie Holiday and written by Crouch/Hathaway.

The Power of Red Lipstick

"If the house is on fire, go on ahead without me.
I'll be right out after I put my lipstick on."
– my mother

I was nine when I began to understand the power of red lipstick.
It had to have some magic to keep my mother inside a burning house.

With my mother, it was always red lips -
Rose of Sharon red for church
Candy Apple red for a day at the park
and on Daddy's payday,
Ox Blood.

She filleted my father with her words,
froze him out with a roll of her eyes,
but on Ox Blood lipstick paydays,
with a slow lean in, a kiss
just barely grazing his lips,
she could reduce the man of the house
to kiddie table stature.

Mother was never more beautiful
than when she sang with Lady Day
playing on the turntable.
Her back supported by the doorframe,
her arms crossed at her breasts,
her long slender fingers holding a cigarette stained Ruby.

Wisps of smoke encircled my mother's head.
She'd take a drag in between measures.
Lady Day wore red lipstick, too.
Though the album cover was in black and white,
I could tell. She had to know
the power of red lipstick.

The greatest gift my mother ever gave me
was an old tube of Blue Flame red lipstick.
It was my sixteenth birthday. My hands were shaking.
I went into the bathroom, sweet and scrubbed-faced.

I came out red-lipped and drunken with the power
of red lipstick. Taller, straighter, hips swaying, eyes rolling.
Blue Flame all day. A drop of gloss in the center of lips slightly parted.
Deeper, slower, metered speech and a throaty laugh.
Glam red, Brick red, Currant red lipstick.
Get the door for me red. Get the cab for me red.
Twelve dozen roses for me red lipstick. My mother knew,
Lady Day knew and I know too,
the power of red lipstick.

The Poet is Freed

I.

A swarm of snapdragons bends itself east
to hear you, *into- the- air- believe- me* woman.
It knows you will pierce verse.

The voices before you—
the first few—they were people,
bad as rhododendron raindrops
in the cathedral. Dangerous
as shards of broken glass.

This boarded-up building
was your chrysalis, until
underneath stars
a blanket of smoke,
the mosaic color of mangoes,
crawled into your mind.

So travel to the edge of jazz barely breathing;
a pocketful of pressed flowers in your torn T-shirt.
Dance in downtown puddles, through the
blues, bird droppings, sweet as
a swarm of snapdragons.
You used to play
he, she
you, me
us
they.

II.

I am walking through this poem
aware of breath and heartbeat.
My footsteps give me away—alternately

right as rhododendron rain then tentatively
tip-toeing on buckling
bridges of language. Forgive me
swarms of snap dragons. Sometimes
a girl needs some pretty piece of language
to rest upon her head like a tiara.
Feed me fragments of mosaic mango.
Sometimes a girl needs a bit of sweet language
she can roll around on her tongue.

Lie to me. Tell me
it is as easy as bending east, as easy as leaving
Little Rock on the next sliver of dawn
to find the edge of jazz barely breathing.
Tell me *No creature ever falls short*
of its own completion. Tell me to piece
together torn bits of language
to make a map to anywhere that is not
boarded up. I want to be dangerous
as shards of broken glass in the mouth.
I want to hear the voices from before the creation
promise me: *No creature ever falls short*
of its own completion; wherever it stands,
*it does not fail to cover the ground.**

*Dogen, a 13th century philosopher.

Upon Waking

Fall

to decline. to descend. to come down suddenly from
an upright position; tumble, collapse; to be wounded
or killed in battle; to become lower, less, weaker;
to lose power, status; do wrong, to yield to
temptation, sin; to be captured;
be directed by chance;
to be divided
(into)

I wouldn't want to fall.
I'd rather walk into love
with eyes wide open.

The robins are returning

The robins are returning
though the wind keeps blowing
and the steely gray skies silhouette
trees that winter has stripped to sticks.

The morning is still until widening
swells of crows burst from rooftops,
like sudden black explosions.

I want to ask the sun:
what do I do when I am lonely –
when I cannot warm my soul, no
matter how close I come to the fire?
How do I fit myself into your embrace
assured that I, too, will rise again?

Chorus of the Nightingale

When the drape of evening descends, the pale moonflowers bloom;
the evening primrose will curtsy in a flourish of pink petticoats;
a contralto chorus of Nightingale will make a fugue of your name,
then find me in the shadows of the sweet chestnut trees.

When gleaming angels' trumpets awaken white in the moonlight,
the sleepy deer will nudge the water lilies about the pond.
The fawn will drink deeply, safely shrouded by the darkness. Come.
The owl need not know who we are. The chattering cricket will not tell.

Before the dawn chorus whistles the morning glory awake.
Before the day lily bathes her face in fresh dew. You will
find me waiting beneath the sweet chestnut trees. Come.

Upon Waking

I awaken to the play of shadows on purple walls
and inhale the dissipating traces of love past:
a scent reminiscent of musk and sandalwood.
The wind's wet breath fogs the window,
driving me deeper beneath the duvet.
The space between his back and the wall
is Petra, the last vestige of safety in tribulation.

These walls intersect in pristine perpendicular angles my eyes chase
to the soft glow of white ceiling. In the periphery, the walls
shimmer like amethyst silk. I recall a book I read as a child
about a woman named Lydia. A seller of purple. A widow woman
who sold dyed fabrics. Silks. Cottons. Linen stained with the life blo
of mollusks. Life blood, clear as crystal. Reflective. Refractive until
kissed by the air. Then a burst of purple. I read somewhere
the ancient dying places are littered with shells to this present day.
The ancient basins lay abandoned with their purple stain.

My love is still sleeping. He mumbles as he rolls to face me. His brea
is warm, sweet. Our syncopated breathing finds a common rhythm.

It is written, for his part in saving Israel, Mordecai went out
from the presence of the king in a mantle of fine linen and purple.
Because Daniel could read the writing on the wall,
Belshazzar clothed him in purple, made him third ruler of the kingd

But I never wore purple.
Lavender once or twice. Muted. Watered down. And now,
he has wrapped me in purple walls. Slipped me between purple shee
Summoned the twilight to dance across my dusky skin.

We were taught God opened Lydia's heart, transforming her.
What did Lydia become, that she was not already?

Through the window, ashen clouds bow to daybreak.
I ignore the insistent rooster. I would chase away the sun
to remain within these purple walls. I am stained purple.

I read of the priests who entered the Holy of Holies long ago.
Once a year, a priest would enter, draw back the veil
which was gathered together with purple cord. Were he
unworthy, he would fall dead. And another would enter.

My love has entered. Confidently brushed aside the veil,
walked the corridor to my innermost chamber to find it dark and empty.
His countenance has brought light. He has bathed me in kisses.
Stripped away my sack cloth and set me on high. Fear has fallen away.
The quiet is filled with the melody of my name.

What has become of Mordecai's mantle? Has the writing changed on
Daniel's wall? And Lydia? Does she rest in her Lord's arms?
Some things we cannot know.

But the ancient dying places, with their shells and stained basins,
these things survive. And purple. The color purple. It remains
in fields of forget-me-nots that bloom in the coolness of morning.

Mid-Day

window blinds slice
the sun into lemon pie wedges
and then splatters them
onto the wall

Psalm of the Sunflower

I am the sunflower
who follows the sun always

hoping
hoping

dark face uncovered
petals peeled back

eager

balanced
on a flexible stem

expecting all I need
is in the light

expecting always
to follow the light.

About the Poet

Antoinette Brim teaches Creative Writing, World Literature and Composition at Pulaski Technical College in North Little Rock, Arkansas. A Cave Canem Fellow and recipient of the Archie D. and Bertha H. Walker Foundation Scholarship to the Fine Arts Work Center in Provincetown, she earned an MFA in Creative Writing/Poetry from Antioch University/Los Angeles. She is also the recipient of a Pushcart Prize nomination. *Psalm of the Sunflower* is her debut poetry collection.